Countries of the World

Ghana

by Lucile Davis

Consultant:
Sam Afrifa-Kyei
Minister
Embassy of Ghana

Bridgestone Books
an imprint of Capstone Press
Mankato, Minnesota

Bridgestone Books are published by Capstone Press
818 North Willow Street, Mankato, Minnesota 56001
http://www.capstone-press.com

Library of Congress Cataloging-in-Publication Data
Davis, Lucile.
    Ghana/by Lucile Davis.
    p. cm.—(Countries of the world)
    Includes bibliographical references (p. 24) and index.
    Summary: An introduction to the geography, history,
natural resources, culture, and people of the west African
country of Ghana.
    ISBN 0-7368-0069-7
    1. Ghana—Juvenile literature. [1. Ghana.] I. Title.
II. Series: Countries of the world (Mankato, Minn.)
DT510.D38   1999
966.7—dc21
                                                    98-3486
                                                      CIP
                                                      AC

Editorial Credits

Martha E. Hillman, editor; James Franklin, cover designer and illustrator;
  Sheri Gosewisch, photo researcher

Photo Credits

John Elk III, 5 (bottom), 6, 14
Michele Burgess, 16
StockHaus Limited, 5 (top)
Unicorn Stock Photos/Florent Flipper, 20
Victor Englebert, cover, 8, 10, 12, 18

Table of Contents

Fast Facts

Name: Republic of Ghana

Capital: Accra

Population: About 18 million

Official Language: English

Religions: Traditional beliefs, Islam, Christianity

Size: 92,098 square miles (238,534 square kilometers)

Ghana is almost as big as the U.S. state of Oregon.

Crops: Cacao, coffee, rice

Maps

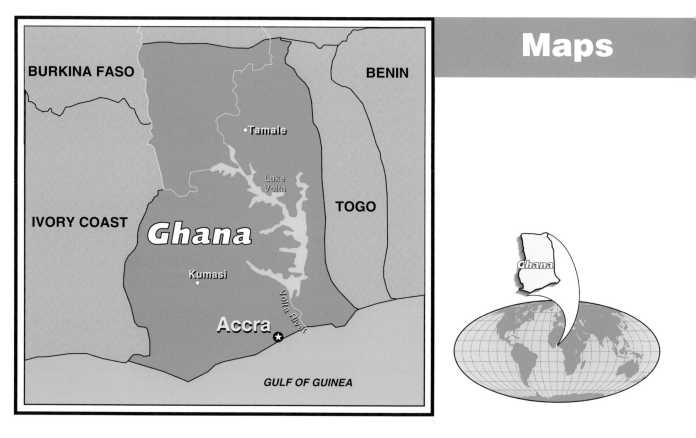

BURKINA FASO

BENIN

•Tamale

Lake Volta

IVORY COAST

TOGO

Ghana

Kumasi

Volta River

Accra

GULF OF GUINEA

Ghana

Flag

Ghana's flag has three stripes and a star. The top stripe is red. Red stands for the blood of people who fought for Ghana. The middle stripe is gold. Gold represents Ghana's wealth. The bottom stripe is green. Green stands for Ghana's forests. The flag has a black star in the middle. The star reminds people of Ghana's freedom.

Currency

The unit of currency in Ghana is the cedi. One hundred pesewas make up one cedi.

In the late 1990s, about 2,300 cedi equaled one U.S. dollar. About 1,600 cedi equaled one Canadian dollar.

The Land of Ghana

Ghana lies on the western coast of Africa. The Gulf of Guinea borders Ghana's shores. The gulf is part of the Atlantic Ocean.

Three types of land cover Ghana. Savannas cover northern Ghana. This flat, grassy land has few trees. Forests stand in central Ghana. Southern Ghana has swamps. The land is wet and spongy.

The Volta River flows through the middle of Ghana. People built a dam on this river. The water in the river backed up behind the dam. This formed Lake Volta. It is the world's fifth-largest lake made by people.

Ghana has a tropical climate. The weather is usually hot and wet. Ghana sometimes receives a lot of rain. The country also has dry periods when little rain falls.

The Volta River flows through the middle of Ghana.

Life at Home

More than 60 percent of Ghanaians live in villages. A village home usually has one room. People build their homes with bricks made of mud and gravel. They construct roofs with palm leaves or long grass.

About 40 percent of Ghanaians live in cities. Accra, Kumasi, and Tamale are large cities in Ghana. Ghanaian cities are similar to North American cities. Some Ghanaians live in houses that look like North American houses. Others live in apartments or in houses similar to village homes.

Families are important to Ghanaians. Families gather for special occasions. Grandparents, aunts, uncles, and cousins often live together in village homes. Family members in cities live farther away from one another.

More than 60 percent of Ghanaians live in villages.

Going to School

Children in Ghana attend grade school for six years. They must go to middle school for three years. Some students continue their education with three years of high school. Students may go on to university after high school.

Students learn reading, writing, math, and English. English is the official language of Ghana. Many students speak native languages at home. Twi (TCHWI-i), Ewe (EH-veh), and Ga (GAH) are some languages.

Children in cities attend schools that are much like North American schools. But some villages do not have school buildings. The government is building more schools in these areas. Teachers are holding school outdoors until they have school buildings. Students sometimes bring their own chairs and tables to outdoor classes.

Students learn reading, writing, math, and English.

Ghanaian Food

Vegetables and fruit are the main foods in Ghana. Ghanaians also eat beans and fish.

Fufu is a common meal. People make fufu by boiling yams, plantains, and cassava roots. Ghanaians mix these foods together. They use their hands to shape the mix into balls. Ghanaians may eat fufu with stew.

Ghanaians make stew with beans. People add tomatoes, peppers, and onions to the stew. They may add meat. People often add chopped peanuts.

Most Ghanaian meals include fruit. People eat bananas, coconuts, and pineapples. They also fry or boil plantains. Plantains look like bananas.

Ghanaians do not eat sweets with most meals. But children sometimes eat freshly cut sugarcane. Sugarcane is a treat.

Ghanaians use their hands to form fufu into balls.

Clothing in Ghana

Ghanaians wear several styles of clothing. Some Ghanaians wear the same type of clothing as people in North America. Others wear traditional clothing.

Some Ghanaians wear ntamas (nn-TAH-mahs). A ntama is a large piece of brightly colored cloth. People wrap ntamas around their bodies.

Ghanaians make most ntamas out of kente (KEN-tuh) cloth. Making kente cloth is a tradition in some villages.

Women spin cotton into thread. They dye the thread bright colors. Weavers make kente cloth with the colorful threads.

Men and boys are weavers. They weave kente cloth in narrow strips. The strips are about five inches (13 centimeters) wide. People sew these strips together to make ntamas.

Men and boys weave kente cloth.

Animals in Ghana

Many animals live in Ghana. Herds of elephants and antelope travel on Ghana's savannas. Lions and hyenas hunt there.

Other animals live in Ghana's tropical forests. Monkeys and chimpanzees make their homes in the trees. Parrots and other birds nest in the forests.

Hippos and crocodiles live in Ghana's swamps. Cobras and other snakes hunt in these wetlands.

Many Ghanaians have settled in areas where animals live. The animals now have less space for their homes. The government of Ghana has set up some areas as animal reserves. People cannot live or hunt on reserves. Animals live there freely.

Lions live on Ghana's savannas.

Sports and Games

Soccer is the most popular sport in Ghana. Ghanaians call soccer football. Many people play soccer. Others watch and cheer for their favorite soccer teams. Ghana's national soccer team is the Black Stars.

Other popular sports in Ghana include boxing and swimming. Many Ghanaians play golf and tennis.

Mancala is one of the world's oldest games. It is a board game played with cups and small objects. Players try to collect the most objects. People throughout Africa play this game.

Ghanaians call the game oware (oh-WAHR-ay). They play oware with 48 beans and 12 cups. Players drop beans into cups and pick them up. They follow a certain pattern. Players try to collect the most beans.

Oware is a board game played in Ghana.

Holidays and Celebrations

Ghanaians celebrate Independence Day on March 6. Ghana won its independence from Great Britain on March 6, 1957. People watch parades and sing Ghana's national song to celebrate Independence Day.

Ghana has many traditional celebrations. These celebrations honor events such as weddings, births, and harvests. People wear their best clothes at celebrations. Some people sing and play drums. Other people dance to the music.

A durbar (DUHR-bah) is an important part of traditional celebrations. A durbar starts with a parade through a village. Leaders wear their best ntamas. Everyone else follows the leaders. They all go to the center of the village. There villagers honor their highest ranking leader.

A durbar is a part of celebrations in Ghana.

Hands on: Play Big Snake

Children in Ghana play a game called big snake. Big snake is a tag game. You can play this game.

What You Need

a group of 8 to 10 friends
a large playing area
several rocks

What You Do

1. Pick one person to be the snake.
2. The snake picks a home area within the playing area. Make a circle around this area with the rocks.
3. The snake comes out of its home and tries to catch the other players. Players that the snake catches join hands with the snake. They become part of the snake's body. The first and last person in the snake's body can catch players.
4. Free players can try to break the snake's body. The snake's body breaks if joined players let go of their hands. The snake's body must return home to rejoin if it breaks.
5. The game ends when all players are part of the snake's body. Pick a new snake and play again.

Learn to Speak Twi

come	bra	(BRAH)
go	koh	(KOH)
good evening	mma adjo	(MAH DWO)
good morning	mma ache	(MAH KYEH)
no	dabe	(DAH-bih)
please	me pawocheo	(MEH pa-WO-kye-wo)
thank you	meda ase	(MEH-da WO-ahs)
today	enne	(EH-neh)
yes	aan	(AH-neh)

Words to Know

reserve (ri-ZURV)—a place people set aside for animals to live

savanna (suh-VAN-uh)—a flat, grassy land with few trees

tradition (truh-DISH-uhn)—a belief, idea, or practice that people continue over many years; older people often teach traditions to younger people.

weave (WEEV)—to pass threads over and under one another; people weave threads into cloth.

Read More

Barnett, Jeanie M. *Ghana.* New York: Chelsea House, 1997.
Brace, Steve. *Ghana.* New York: Thomson Learning, 1995.

Useful Addresses and Internet Sites

Embassy of Ghana
3512 International Drive NW
Washington, DC 20008

Ghana High Commission
1 Clemow Ave
Ottawa, Ontario K1S 2A9
Canada

Excite Travel: Ghana
http://www.city.net/countries/ghana

The Republic of Ghana Web Page
http://www.ghana.gov.gh

Index